World of Farming

Food from Farms

Nancy Dickmann

Heinemann Library
Chicago, Illinois

www.capstonepub.com
Visit our website to find out more information about Heinemann-Raintree books.

To order:

☎ Phone 800-747-4992

💻 Visit www.capstonepub.com to browse our catalog and order online.

Edited by Siân Smith, Nancy Dickmann, and Rebecca Rissman
Designed by Joanna Hinton-Malivoire
Picture research by Mica Brancic
Production by Victoria Fitzgerald
Originated by Capstone Global Library Ltd
Printed in the United States of America in Eau Claire, Wisconsin.
113017   010961RP

15 14 13
10 9 8 7 6 5 4 3

Library of Congress Cataloging-in-Publication Data
Dickmann, Nancy.
  Food from farms / Nancy Dickmann.—1st ed.
    p. cm.—(World of farming)
  Includes bibliographical references and index.
  ISBN 978-1-4329-3936-6 (hc)—ISBN 978-1-4329-3943-4 (pb)
  1. Farms—Miscellanea—Juvenile literature. 2. Food crops—Juvenile literature. 3. Food animals—Juvenile literature. I. Title. II. Series: Dickmann, Nancy. World of farming.
  S519.D53 2010
  630—dc22
                                      2009051569

Acknowledgements
We would like to thank the following for permission to reproduce photographs: Photolibrary pp.**4** (Cultura/Bill Sykes), **5** (Hemis/Bertrand Gardel), **6** (Index Stock Imagery/Inga Spence), **7** (imagebroker.net/ Martin Moxter), **8** (age fotostock/Emilio Ereza), **9** (imagebroker.net/Hans Zaglitsch), **10** (Robert Harding Travel/Ken Gillham), **11** (Fresh Food Images/ Gerrit Buntrock), **12** (Index Stock Imagery/Lynn Stone), **13** (Novastock Novastock), **14** (Hemis/Philippe Renault), **15** (LOOK-foto/Juergen Richter), **16** (Imagestate RM/Mark Henley), **17** (Johner RF/Johner Bildbyra), **18** (White/Andrew Olney), **19** (Cuboimages/Alfio Garozzo), **20** (Glow Images), **21** (Stockbroker/Monkey Business Images Ltd), **22** (Johner RF/Johner Bildbyra), **23 top** (LOOK-foto/Juergen Richter), **23 bottom** (Stockbroker/ Monkey Business Images Ltd).

Front cover photograph of a farm stand with an assortment of summer fruits and vegetables reproduced with permission of iStockPhoto (© Jack Puccio). Back cover photograph of a man hand milking a cow in Normandy, France reproduced with permission of Photolibrary (Fresh Food Images/ Gerrit Buntrock).

The publisher would like to thank Dee Reid, Diana Bentley, and Nancy Harris for their invaluable help with this book.

Every effort has been made to contact copyright holders of material reproduced in this book. Any omissions will be rectified in subsequent printings if notice is given to the publishers.

Contents

What Is a Farm?

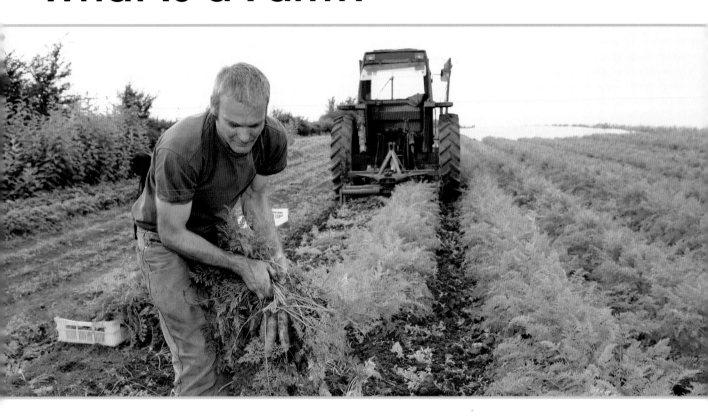

A farm is a place where food is grown.

Farmers sell the food for people to eat.

Plants for Food

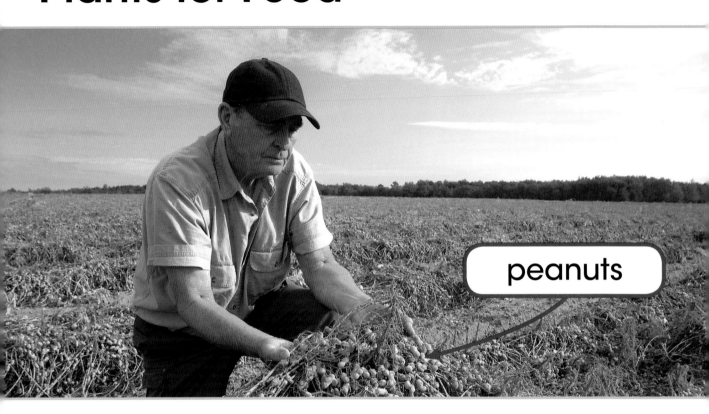

peanuts

Farmers grow plants for us to eat.

Sweet corn grows on a farm.

potatoes

Potatoes grow on a farm.

bananas

Fruit grows on a farm.

Animals for Food

Farmers keep animals that give us food.

Beef and milk come from cows.

Bacon and ham come from pigs.

eggs

Meat and eggs come from chickens.

Getting Food from Farms

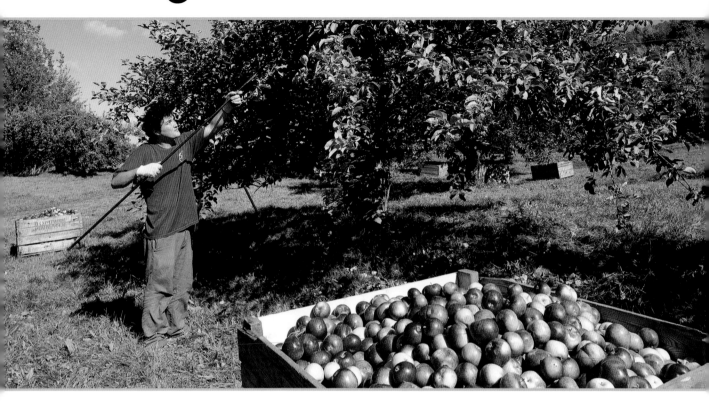

Farmers pick food when it is ready to eat.

The food is packed to keep it safe.

hot apple cider

Some food from farms is made into other food.

wheat

bread

Wheat can be made into bread.

Oranges can be made into juice.

Milk can be made into cheese.

Trucks take the food to stores.

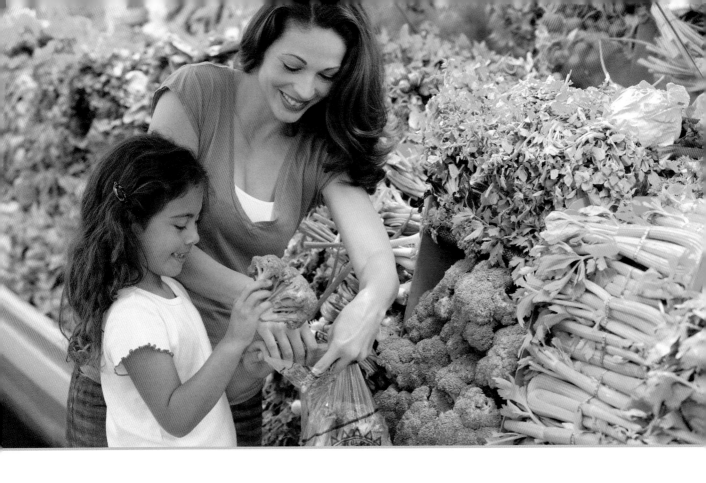

We buy food at the store.

Can You Remember?

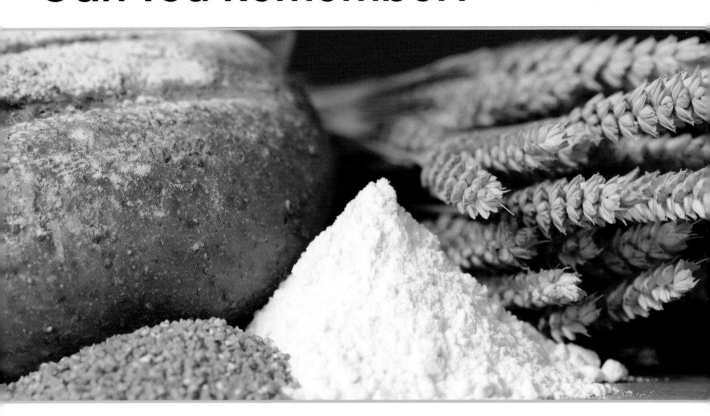

What is bread made from?

Answer on page 24

Picture Glossary

pack to put something into boxes. We pack food so that it is easier to move it from place to place.

store place where we can buy things. Some stores sell food for us to eat.

Index

Answer to question on page 22: Bread is made from wheat. First wheat is ground into flour. Then flour is used to make bread.

Note to Parents and Teachers

Before reading:
Ask the children if they have ever visited a farm. Ask them what food they think grows on farms. Make a list together. Can they tell you which foods are fruits, vegetables, meats, or grains? Explain that there are farms all over the world. Farms in different places can grow different kinds of food. Encourage children to think about the kinds of food that may come from other countries and how this food gets to them. For example, bananas (shown on page 9) are grown in hot countries and are transported on airplanes and trucks.

After reading:
• Ask the children to brainstorm all the different kinds of fruits they can think of. Ask the children if they know what kinds of fruits grow in their country. Do they know where the other kinds grow? For example, do bananas grow where they live? If not, do they know why? Look at a map and talk about where in the world different kinds of fruits grow. Talk about how some fruit has to travel a long way for many people to eat it.

• Ask the children if they know what flour is made from. Show them some wheat stalks and some grains of wheat and explain how grains are ground to make flour. See how many foods they can think of that need flour. They could do a survey to see which of these foods each class member likes best and then make a tally chart together.